‑/₂₂/₀/

MW00830006

THE TOWER

WITH ~~~~
AND ADMIRATION
MATTHEW

A · T · L

THE
TOWER

Matthew Maguire

LOS ANGELES
SUN & MOON PRESS
1993

Sun & Moon Press
A Program of The Contemporary Arts Educational Project, Inc.
a nonprofit corporation
6026 Wilshire Boulevard, Los Angeles, California 90036

This edition first published in paperback in 1993 by Sun & Moon Press
10 9 8 7 6 5 4 3 2 1
FIRST EDITION
This book was made possible, in part, through an operational grant from
the Andrew W. Mellon Foundation and through contributions to
The Contemporary Arts Educational Project, Inc.,
a nonprofit corporation

Cover: April Gornik
Reprinted by permission of the artist

LIBRARY OF CONGRESS CATALOGING IN PUBLICATION DATA
Maguire, Matthew
The Tower
p. cm — (American Theater in Literature Program)
ISBN: 1-55713-133-3
I. Title. II. Series.
811'.54—dc20

Printed in the United States of America on acid-free paper.

ACKNOWLEDGMENTS

The Tower was conceived as an opera with music by Glenn Branca, a contemporary vision of the Tower of Babel. Glenn and I intended the opera to be scored for orchestra and five singers. Since the medium was new for both of us, we planned the process as a series of productions serving as studies for the larger work. Robert Stearns at the Walker Art Center commissioned the first phase of the project, a stage play with incidental music, co-produced with the Illusion Theatre and Creation Production Company. When John Killacky began his tenure at the Walker, he ensured that the play would continue. The first workshops of the play were held at the Illusion Theatre in October of 1987 and subsequently at the New City Theatre in January of 1988. It received its premiere at the Illusion in March, 1989. The second step was a chamber version that Creation Production Company produced as a work-in-progress with Home for Contemporary Theatre and Art in May, 1989. Then a site-specific variation entitled "Babel On Babylon" was created for Belvedere Castle in Central Park, commissioned by Anne Hamburger and co-produced with En Garde Arts. Subsequently, the Meet the Composer / Readers' Digest Commissioning Program awarded Glenn and me commissions to write the opera. With the assistance of a McKnight Fellowship, the Playwrights Center, and the Minnesota Opera's New Music Theatre Ensemble, I spent two months in Minneapolis working on rewriting the play as libretto. Working with singers was enlightening, as was a subsequent workshop at New Dramatists aided by the direction of Roger Ames. The most recent 'variation on the theme' was a solo, "Babel Stories," which I performed in February, 1990. The Creation production of the solo was supported by Casey Childs and Primary Stages. The reason for my extensive thanks is that the current text is the result of multiple productions.

My deep thanks to those already mentioned as well as to Douglas Messerli, Michael Robins and Bonnie Morris, John Kazanjian, Mary Ewald, Brian Faker, Ki Gottberg, Randy Rollison, April Gornik (for her beautiful drawing), Susan McClary and Elana Greenfield (for their incisive criticisms), New Dramatists, Mac Wellman (for introducing this play to Douglas Messerli), David Moore, Cynthia Gehrig, Sara Burstein, Jerome Foundation, Ben Krywocz, Rabbi Barry Holt of the Jewish Theological Seminary (for his guidance and encouragement), Jennifer McDowall (for her multiple roles), Tony Kushner (for his encouragement), Andreas Nowara (to whom the original production was dedicated), Joe Fyfe, Joe Gallant, Mark Lutwak, Gerald Clarke, Clinton Fisher, Mike Gladstone, Martin Hauser, Anne Hemenway, Joumana Rizk, Stephen Sherrill, Dorothea Tanning, and the Creation Board (for their moral and financial support), my parents Joan and Bruce Maguire , Glenn Branca (for his beautiful score), and special thanks to my partner, Susan Mosakowski (for her artistry and support).

The Tower premiered at the Illusion Theater in Minneapolis, March 1, 1989, Michael Robins and Bonnie Morris, Producing Directors. The production was a co-production of the Walker Art Center, the Illusion Theater and Creation Production Company, directed by the author.

Cast:

RUTH	Mary McDevitt
JACOB	Jefferson Slinkard
DR. RAFEL	Alfred Harrison
DR. AMEK	Megan Grundy
DR. ZABI	Marysue Moses

Music	Glenn Branca
Choreography	Susan Mosakowski
Set Design	Dean Holzman and
	Matthew Maguire
Light Design	Jeff Bartlett
Costume Design	Katherine Maurer
Assistant Director	Walton Stanley
Dramaturg	Rabbi Barry Holtz

The chamber version of *The Tower* was presented at Home for Contemporary Theatre and Art in New York City in May, 1989.

Cast:

RUTH	Shellye Broughton
JACOB	Anthony Lee
DR. RAFEL	Michael Ryan
DR. AMEK	Isabel Sáez
DR. ZABI	Kazuki Takase

Set Design	Joe Fyfe
Light Design	Pat Dignan

Scene 1: Now the whole earth had one language and few words.

Scene 2: And as men migrated from the east, they found a plain in the land of Shinar and settled there.

Scene 3: And they said to one another, "Come, let us make bricks, and burn them thoroughly." And they had brick for stone, and bitumen for mortar.

Scene 4: Then they said, "Come, let us build ourselves a city, and a tower with its top in the heavens, and let us make a name for ourselves lest we be scattered abroad upon the face of the whole earth."

Scene 5: And the LORD came down to see the city and the tower, which the sons of men had built.

Scene 6: And the LORD said, "Behold, they are one people, and they all have one language; and this is only the beginning of what they will do; and nothing they propose to do will now be impossible for them.

Scene 7: Come, let us go down, and there confuse their language, that they may not understand one another's speech."

Scene 8: So the LORD scattered them abroad from there over the face of all the earth, and they left off building the city.

Scene 9: Therefore its name was called Babel, because the LORD confused the language of all the earth; and from there the LORD scattered them abroad over the face of all the earth.

THE TOWER

Characters:

> RUTH, Fighting for her life on the operating table.
>
> JACOB, Her husband.
>
> DR. RAFEL, Male, the brilliant but autocratic chief surgeon.
>
> DR. AMEK, Female, surgeon, an advocate of patient's rights.
>
> DR. ZABI, Male or female, surgeon, a cautious careerist.
>
> A small chorus that plays nurses, prisoners, a tribe of Bedouins, Babylonian masons and a squadron of angels.

Time:

> From the beginning to the end of a delicate and dangerous surgery.

Place:

> *There are three settings that must flow one into another:*

> ¶ An operating room. The walls glow with the constellations of a winter sky at midnight. The medical machinery appears oversized and ominous.
>
> ¶ Ruth and Jacob's living room in flashback: where unfold the events which lead to her operation;
>
> ¶ A nightmarish zone of prison cells in global crisis spots.

Prologue:

> *The sounds of the operating room are heard as the surgeons prepare for a dangerous emergency operation on RUTH's mouth. The surgeons and nurses dance stiffly, oddly, and repetitively through their preparations.*

SCENE 1

One Language and Few Words

¶ THE OPERATING THEATRE

> *The operation is about to begin. An argument has erupted over* JACOB's *second thoughts about* RUTH's *surgery.*

JACOB: Listen to me! This is not—

DR. RAFEL: Without this operation your wife won't make it.

JACOB: Listen to me! Surgery's not going—

DR. RAFEL: —I'm the doctor here, not—

JACOB: You don't understand. You have to—

DR. RAFEL: —No, you don't understand, your wife could die.

DR. AMEK: Hear him out.

DR. RAFEL: Get him out of here!

JACOB: I'm staying.

DR. RAFEL: No!

JACOB: You agreed.

DR. RAFEL: No!

DR. AMEK: Dr. Rafel…

DR. RAFEL: The rules strictly forbid—

DR. AMEK: —We've seen loved ones bring a patient through.

DR. RAFEL: NO! I'm the chief surgeon!

JACOB: Maybe surgery's not the answer.

DR. RAFEL: And why not?

JACOB: The nightmares.

DR. AMEK: Nightmares?

JACOB: Yes, of prison cells, every—

DR. RAFEL: —Psycho-babble.

JACOB: They're the cause—

DR. RAFEL: It's a surgical problem. And she'll die if we don't start.

JACOB: I'll allow it only if I stay.

DR. ZABI: He's right, Doctor, you've got to have his consent.

DR. RAFEL: He already signed.

JACOB: I'll hit you with malpractice.

> *A long pause while RAFEL considers, then imperiously nods his consent.*

DR. RAFEL: Begin.

DR. AMEK: Prep.

DR. ZABI: Starting prep.

RUTH: Jacob?

JACOB: I understand.

DR. ZABI: Pressure?

DR. AMEK: One ten over seventy.

> *The operating lights pulse.*

RUTH: Jacob…

JACOB: Shhhhhhhhh…

RUTH: My mouth…

JACOB: I know… shhhhhhhh… don't talk.

RUTH: … so scared…

JACOB: Shhhhh… still… [*pause*]. Breathe deep, breathe deep, that's it…

> *The sounds of hissing gas and deep breathing combine and rise in volume. Lights fade except for the blue of the operating table's glass top with its neon outline of* RUTH. *We glimpse a desert landscape of shifting sands and swirling skies as the stage changes to a nightmare version of* RUTH *and* JACOB's *bedroom as a prison cell.*

❡ THE PRISON

> RUTH *and* JACOB *are sleeping.* RUTH *is having a nightmare. Prisoners in black-striped uniforms advance relentlessly, holding out a uniform they press upon her. Each of them sings in a different language. Flashes of headlines from crisis points around the world fill the air aurally and visually.*

> RUTH *wakes up screaming. The prisoners vanish.*

JACOB: [*shaking her*] Ruth, Ruth, Ruth! It's all right, it's only a dream.

RUTH: It's the same one, over and over and over and over and—

JACOB: It's all right, it's all right.

RUTH: [*dazed*] a cell… a prison cell.

¶ THE HOUSE

> *A simple painted drop can indicate the house, perhaps a dollhouse-like cutaway of all the rooms.* RUTH *and* JACOB *read the Sunday paper.*

RUTH: Jacob…

JACOB: Hmmmm…

RUTH: Did you read this story?

JACOB: Hmm?

RUTH: This story.

JACOB: What's it say?

RUTH: They found the original site of the Tower of Babel.

JACOB: My middle name.

RUTH: These people almost made it to paradise. It's giving me the shivers.

JACOB: Ruth, it's Sunday. Can you rest your awesome digging for one day?

RUTH: This scientist says they felt an unnatural heat rising from the earth...

JACOB: You wanna feel some unnatural heat—come 'ere...

RUTH: She says the ruins are still seething with heat and ready to erupt to heaven all over again...

JACOB: That's what I'm saying, now come onnnnnn....

RUTH: Listen, here's the original story, "Now the whole earth had one language—

> JACOB *chases her, laughing, around the house. The laughter becomes orgasmically coloratura. Blackout.*

¶ THE BEDOUIN DANCE

> *Two Bedouins with long flowing azure veils dance an ancient tribal dance.*

SCENE 2

THE SOUND OF A DISTANT TRAIN

¶ THE HOUSE

Part 1—Afterglow (Bliss and Babelonia)

RUTH: "And they said to one another, 'Come, let us make bricks, and burn them thoroughly.' And they had brick for stone, and bitumen for mortar"… Bitumen? What's bitumen?

JACOB: It's a lost word, Ruth.

RUTH: Words can't get lost.

JACOB: Old 'woids' never die, they just mutate.

RUTH: [*Shrieks*] Aiiiiiiiiiiiii……. Here it is! A footnote! "Bitumen"—it's tar, or asphalt, earthy pitchy stuff like in bituminous coal—what they had for mortar.

JACOB: [*gasping*] Ohhh… "bitumen," of course, why didn't you say so! [*pause*] Ruth… I feel sort of earthy and pitchy after that big excitement.

RUTH: Oh you poor dear, come here…

Part 2—A Week Later (The Long Hand of the Lord)

RUTH: Oh no! Jacob! I'm losing it again. There goes the mouth. Oh my Gaw…ddd.

> JACOB *molds her mouth, coaching her through her words.*

JACOB: That's it. That's it…

JACOB and RUTH: OH…MAH…YEE…GAH…DUH!

> *She snaps out of it.*

RUTH: Ahhhhhh…

JACOB: Ruth, what is going on with your speech?

RUTH: I might need an operation on my mouth, Jacob.

JACOB: It's a week now and it's getting worse. If you're working on something I want to help. Why is this happening?

RUTH: [*pause*] Are we ever going to move?

JACOB: Where do you want to move to?

The Tower

    In the distance is heard the sound of a train whistle, mournful, haunting, beautiful. Out of it grows the sound of the Angel Choir, largo mysterioso. JACOB *is unaware of the sound.* RUTH *is entranced.*

RUTH: To the tower... the tower... the tower...

    JACOB *fades away and* RUTH *is isolated.*

RUTH: I want to build. I want to build a tower whose top reaches unto heaven. A tower so high that when I stand at the top and look down a palm tree below will seem no larger than a grasshopper. I dream of building and I build of dreaming. I am the woman of brick, embedded in this tower of brick, baked hard and laid with slime. I will always live in these bricks. Even after they decompose I will hover above this site and trace in ghostly memories the endless repetition of the bricks. I love the bricks, baked hard and burned to a burning. Each brick bearing its own story. This is the brick that is laid as the hawk swoops, and this is the brick that is laid as the mortar runs dry, and this is the brick that is laid as a wracking cough seizes the chest. And I live in each one. I am the woman of the bricks. I'm building the tower because when it cracks the gates of heaven then every story of every brick will be released at once.

¶ THE BEDOUIN DANCE, *reprise*

    Seven Bedouins enter dancing. A harness drops in and flies RUTH *above the dancing Bedouins. They pitch a tent in the middle of the room. Winds whip the flaps. The room is covered with images of palm trees. Images of trains crossfade—long camel trains and early nineteenth century locomotives. As the Bedouins lead RUTH from her flying position onto the operating table they are eclipsed by the surgeons.*

¶ THE OPERATING THEATRE

RAFEL: What's the pressure?

AMEK: Eighty over fifty—dropping.

ZABI: Change the anesthetic. Stabilize her. Fast!

RAFEL: Scalpel. No! Not that one!

AMEK: Tubing in… Suction.

RAFEL: X-ray shows the shadow here.

ZABI: No, look at the CAT scan. It's deeper.

RAFEL: Lost it. Vital signs.

AMEK: Pulse getting rapid. Respiration's… twenty-two…

ZABI: Losing a lot of blood.

RAFEL: Transfuse one unit.

ZABI: She's not going to make it.

RAFEL: Transfuse the unit goddamnit!

ZABI: Still losing.

RAFEL: Transfuse second unit... Add...

ZABI: Adding!

AMEK: Ligate?

RAFEL: NO! Pressure?

AMEK: Dropping seventy over forty. Ligate?

RAFEL: NO! Now back off! Scalpel.

JACOB: [*rushing to her side*] Breathe deep, breathe deep, that's it.

> *The operating table tilts and rises to an unreal height.*

RUTH: The scene is an operating theatre. I am on the table. Dreaming.

JACOB: The scene is an operating theatre. I am on the dreaming.

ZABI: The scene is a table. I am the dreaming.

AMEK: The scene is a dreaming.

RAFEL: The scene is on the dreaming table dreaming table dreaming.

RUTH, JACOB, RAFEL, AMEK, ZABI: [*absolute unison*] I am on the table. Dreaming.

A weaving chorale of growing excitement

RUTH: I am on the table. Dreaming. JACOB: The scene is an operating theatre.

RAFEL: I am on the table. AMEK: The scene is a dreaming.

ZABI: I am the dreaming.

RUTH: I am on the table. Dreaming. JACOB: The scene is an operating theatre.

RAFEL: I am on the table. AMEK: The scene is a dreaming.

ZABI: I am the dreaming.

RUTH: Dreaming. JACOB: The scene is.

RAFEL: On the table dreaming table dreaming. AMEK: Dreaming.

ZABI: I am.

The Tower

RUTH: I am   JACOB: [*delayed*] I am

        AMEK: Dreaming.

RUTH: I am   RAFEL: [*delayed*] I am

        AMEK: Dreaming.

RUTH: I am   AMEK: [*delayed*] I am

        RAFEL: Dreaming.

RUTH: I am   ZABI: [*delayed*] I am

RUTH, JACOB, RAFEL, AMEK, ZABI: Dreaming.

RUTH: I   JACOB: I

        RAFEL: I

AMEK: I   ZABI: I

Driving Agitato

RAFEL: I hear my heart beating, booming in my ears.

AMEK: I hear the sound of the scalpel cutting my flesh.

RUTH: Jacob! The doctors are all speaking with my voice.

JACOB: Yes… my voice…

25

RUTH: No! My voice.

AMEK: You have many voices.

RUTH: All my voices.

AMEK: We are your many voices.

Speak in unison

RUTH, JACOB, RAFEL, AMEK, ZABI: We are your many
voices.

Pause

RUTH: All my voices.

Pause

ZABI: Speaking at once.

RUTH: All my voices	JACOB: Divided
RAFEL: All my	AMEK: Voices

ZABI: Speaking at once.

RUTH, JACOB, RAFEL, AMEK, ZABI: Ohhhh!

RUTH: Oh my God, you're all speaking my mind. I must be
dying!

26

Rapid echoes, like dominos

JACOB: Dying.

RAFEL: Dying.

AMEK: Dying.

ZABI: Dying.

Counterpoint of decays and crests

RUTH: Dying   JACOB: Dying

RAFEL: Dying   AMEK: Dying

ZABI: Dying

AMEK: If you want to live, concentrate!

RUTH: Ruth, my name is Ruth!

ZABI: There's no need to fear, you never lose your name.

JACOB: The letters that make the name are set in bone.

RUTH: I am my name and when I drift it will anchor me.

AMEK: What will the pain be like when the scalpel cuts?

ZABI: Am I curious?

AMEK: My nerves are screaming.

RUTH: Will I ever stop climbing the face of this tower?

RAFEL: Is the face of this tower malignant?

AMEK: No! It's an open face yearning for paradise.

RAFEL: No! A tower is a tower.

RUTH: I'm sure it's all a mistake—must've used the wrong word.

JACOB: But when?

RAFEL: At the pinnacle.

AMEK: Am I at the top of the tower?

RUTH: [*firm, and strangely assured*] NO. When I reach the top of the tower I will hear the sound of a distant train.

RAFEL: I remember that. How do I remember that?

AMEK: Have I been here before?

ZABI: Oh yes. Many times.

RAFEL: You could almost say you've always been here, like a moth circling a flame.

ZABI: You keep diving into the flame and immolating yourself.

RAFEL: That's why you're on the operating table.

RAFEL, AMEK, ZABI, JACOB: Don't you remember?

Hysterically grasping at straws

RUTH: I'll tell the nurse I'm weeping for my memory, not the pain—I'll remember—resist the flame as I circle... [*pause*] But in what language?

AMEK: What language am I speaking?

ZABI: Can I move my mouth?

RAFEL: Can I make my mouth migrate?

AMEK: Which way is the tower?

Driving Agitato

RAFEL: Follow the heat.

ZABI: Always remember that.

RAFEL: Follow the heat. Move towards the heat. But do not burn yourself.

JACOB: Move   RAFEL: Follow

AMEK: To the heat.   ZABI: The heat.

RAFEL: And keep moving. Stay in motion.

JACOB: Forget the doctor, forget your amnesia, keep moving.

RAFEL: When in trouble speed up and bare your teeth.

AMEK: Or sing a Requiem for the heat.

Gregorian Chant

RAFEL, AMEK, ZABI, JACOB: Sanctus, Sanctus, Sanctus.

Long Pause

RUTH: It is so still.

JACOB: Listen! Do you hear that sound? Is it the voice of God?

RUTH: [*jubilant*] It's the sound of a distant train.

¶ THE PRISON

> RUTH'S *nightmare recurs, thrusting her into a prison
> yard where a radio broadcast is blaring.*

The London Times. Dateline Belfast. The Irish Republican
Army is engulfed in a serious internal dispute because its most
ruthless unit has refused the leadership's order to disband. The
renegade unit coordinated the bombing of the annual memo-
rial service for soldiers killed in the two World Wars at
Enniskillen in County Fermanagh. The attack killed eleven ci-

vilians and provoked worldwide condemnation of the guerrillas.

> *In the background is heard the sound of riots and the
> Babel text from Genesis in Gaelic.* RUTH *witnesses prison-
> ers cross the yard carrying their prison bars before them. They
> sing.*

The Prisoner's Song

We are prisoners on this globe
Condemned alive like Job.
That's why we agree
On the ideology
Of bricks and bitumen.
Building, building, building, is our destiny.
From constant war and chaos we long to be free

SCENE 3

THE IDEOLOGY OF BRICKS AND BITUMEN

¶ THE HOUSE

> *As* JACOB *enters,* RUTH *is rolling a Babylonian brick kiln across the stage, thick smoke pouring out its chimney.*

JACOB: Ruth, why do I keep finding bricks in the oven?

RUTH: I thought we could use some more ruffage in our diet, dear.

JACOB: Does this have anything to do with your obsession with that tower?

RUTH: No, for God's sake, no. Don't worry. I forgot all about that. [*directly to the audience as co-conspirators*] They're not sun-dried bricks but substantial kiln-fired bricks of great durability.

JACOB: Who are you talking to? Are you hearing voices?

RUTH: No, no, just chatting with my guardian angel, darling.

JACOB: There's something veiled about your tone, and there's got to be over two thousand bricks out there.

The sound of the Angel Choir is heard.

RUTH: [*entranced*] One thousand, nine hundred and ninety-six.

¶ THE BRICK DANCE

> *Babylonian workers enter with hods of bricks and the brick dance begins, weaving flowing patterns with the bricks.*

¶ THE OPERATING THEATRE

RAFEL: Vital signs.

AMEK: Stabilized.

RAFEL: She's passed the crisis. You've got to leave.

JACOB: I'm staying.

RAFEL: Our policy doesn't—

JACOB: I'm not leaving her.

ZABI: He seems to help her.

AMEK: I agree, absolutely.

RAFEL: All right then—for now.

33

pause

JACOB: Her eye motion's so rapid—why?

　　　RUTH'S *reality intersects with that of the surgeons'.*

RUTH: I'm at the top of the tower.

AMEK: This anesthetic's giving her dreams.

RUTH: No. I'm in the "room… one… passes… through."

JACOB: I see.

RUTH: Built of blue bricks inlaid with bulls and dragons. The bulls are yellow with manes of lapis lazuli and the dragons white and crested with a shimmering light.

JACOB: It seems she's trying to leave the table.

RUTH: Hold me… I'm frightened!

ZABI: Secure the restraints.

RUTH: Jacob!

JACOB: Her eyes are…

　　　He's too mesmerized to finish. The two realities begin to blur.

RUTH: Like black pearls...

JACOB, RAFEL, AMEK, ZABI: You're talking crazy—stop it! Please!

RUTH: Oh Jacob, I don't want to die!

JACOB, RAFEL, AMEK: You're not!

RUTH: Please tell the Doctor, tell her.

JACOB, AMEK: We know, we're doing everything, it'll be over soon, just hang on.

RUTH: I love you.

RUTH: I love you.   JACOB: Love

RAFEL: Love   AMEK: You

ZABI: You.

JACOB: I know, Love, I love you, just hang on, breathe deep, breathe deep, that's it.

> *Suddenly they are struck by a revolutionary fervor as if they were in a secret meeting of a radical cell planning a revolt.*

RAFEL: And they said to one another.

RUTH: Is my mouth burning?

AMEK: Burning.

RAFEL: Why do we not move from this desert?

AMEK: It's not a desert.

RUTH: It's my mouth.

RAFEL: And it's storming heaven.

RUTH: Who is speaking?

RAFEL, AMEK, ZABI, JACOB: If build we do not, then burnt we will be.

RUTH: Yes!

RAFEL, AMEK, ZABI, JACOB: And they said to one another:

RUTH: Yes!

RAFEL, AMEK, ZABI, JACOB: Rise up!

RUTH: Yes.

RAFEL, AMEK, ZABI, JACOB: Rise Up!

RUTH: YES!

ZABI: Build a tower.

RUTH, JACOB, RAFEL, AMEK, ZABI: YES!

RUTH: My mouth is a kiln.

RAFEL, ZABI: I hear the bricks sing as they rise up.

AMEK, JACOB: And the right of revolt—

RUTH: Is embedded in the tower of my mouth.

¶ THE PRISON

The New York Times. Dateline Lima. A clash in the Upper Huallaga River Valley of Peru has left 15 guerrillas of the leftist Shining Path movement and two soldiers dead, the army reported today. Nearly 20,000 people have died in this seemingly endless struggle.

> *In the background is heard the Babel text in a Peruvian dialect. The prisoners walk the yard, angry and jostling. Trapping* RUTH *against the bars they force a uniform upon her. They sing.*

The Uniform Song

> We're caught in every corner of this earth.
> We're forced to wear these uniforms from birth.
> We're from Belfast and Nicaragua,
> Johannesburg, Miami, and the Gaza.

Matthew Maguire

We have no means to profit
And so our lives are forfeit
in the archipelago corporate.

SCENE 4

A Tower With its Top in the Heavens

¶ THE HOUSE

JACOB: Can you imagine a conspiracy to take over heaven? You'd have to have meetings, and codes, and secret handshakes…

RUTH: What are you driving at, Jacob?

JACOB: You ever think about that sort of stuff?

RUTH: I think the amount of conspiracy reported in daily life is vastly exaggerated.

JACOB: Well… would you happen to be harboring any secret plans?

RUTH: WHAT THE HELL IS GOING ON HERE? YOU FIND SOME LONG JOHN SLIVER DOLL IN THE CLOSET, OR WHAT?!!!

JACOB: Now hold on dear, I'm not accusing you of anything. I just got this feeling there's something you're thinking I don't know about…

RUTH: Of course, I have a secret life. Everyone has a secret life. For Christ sakes it's only natural. Some people have plenty of 'em. Now bugger off!

JACOB: All right, Ruth, I'll be in the garden if there's anything you want to talk about.

> *After* RUTH *is sure he's gone she starts laughing. At first she's just chuckling about her word play but soon she's out of control.*

RUTH: Bugger off, that's a good one, Yah ha ha,
bugger…off, Ya Ha,
Buh Ga..Roo, Yo, HO, HA, HO, HA,
BOO GA ROOO NEE, YA, YA, YA YA,
YA, YA, YA YA,
> *[scared to death]*
JACOB!!!!!

¶ THE OPERATING THEATRE

> JACOB *and the surgeons enter, each with their own operating table on wheels, and carom like bumper cars around the operating room, spinning* RUTH *with them.*

> *Giddy joking punning erotic euphoric badinage*

RAFEL: The scene's an operating theatre. I'm on the table.

Laughing at my fears.

RUTH: I hear my heart beating, booming in my ears.

AMEK: I hear the scalpel cutting my flesh.

RUTH: I hear all my voices focus and mesh.

ZABI: I hear conversations.

RAFEL: Altercations of the surgeons and their nations.

RUTH: Everything I hear is building a tower over my head.

RAFEL: Paradise at the pinnacle.

RAFEL, AMEK: And the tower grows higher.

RAFEL, AMEK, JACOB: As I climb in sweet dread.

RUTH: You won't catch me thinking twice,
      I'm climbing to Paradise.

Chasing riddles

ZABI: It seems that the wind is getting louder, or is it the high
      whine of a drill? The wild and woesome whine of a
      winter wind whipping through the weaving wheel.

AMEK: "W!" Is the answer in the letter "W?"

RUTH: "W"—West, we wander… "L"—Listen, to my lungs laboring…
"D" Dying.
Am I dying?

RAFEL: Of course I'm dying.

ZABI: And I've died many times before.

RAFEL: "T"—Time, counting the pulse.

An eroticon

RAFEL: My throbbing heart.

AMEK: So warm.

ZABI: So sticky.

JACOB: So exciting.

RUTH: So vibrating, like a hummingbird in the genitals.

RUTH: You won't catch me thinking twice,
I'm climbing to Paradise.

Rapid-fire capriccio

AMEK: Is the doctor speaking Babel?

ZABI: Who, that one?

RAFEL: The funny one.

JACOB: She's singing in Greek she's at the peak.

RUTH: She's teasing me!

RAFEL: She's building the walls of the tower.

AMEK: Is the tower evil?

JACOB: It's a glorious thing.

RAFEL: Like a pinnacle of flame.

JACOB: Around which we huddle eon after eon.

RAFEL: A point of flame.

ZABI: Flame baking brick, building breathtaking "B."

RUTH, JACOB, RAFEL, AMEK, ZABI: Building, building, building.

AMEK: BREATH. Don't forget to breathe.

RUTH: Me?

RAFEL: No, you.

AMEK: You comic Sumerians.

ZABI: Babel on, Babylon.

RUTH: You won't catch me thinking twice,
     I'm climbing to Paradise.

Voluptuous and abandoned

RUTH: If I die, I die lost in the alphabet.

AMEK: Swimming and swooning in sweat.

ZABI: If in space or in mind.

RUTH: No tongue has defined.

AMEK: And if the Tower's in my mind, can I hide it from the
     Lord?

Holy rolling revelations

RUTH: Is that him behind that blue mask?

ZABI: Mask! Yes! "M," the mastical mystical musical mask of
     "M."

RUTH: Oh my God, I'm being born again and there's bricks
     everywhere!

Lush and slow

ZABI: And the music is so sweet.

RAFEL: This sound. All these sounds.

AMEK: They drew me here. They break my heart.

ZABI: The music.

JACOB: Swept on elocusic currents of music.

RAFEL: The music cuts to the bone and sets me free.

JACOB: Ain't no lies in the bones.

RAFEL: In the free fall of the bones
        lies the song of an alphabet.

AMEK: The language of my body.

RUTH: The babel of my body.
        You won't catch me thinking twice,
        I'm climbing to Paradise.

Time Traveling

RUTH *hears the Angel Choir echoing in the whistle of a distant train. She wraps herself in a huge azure veil which drops down from the grid and fills the stage, its lines coming to a focus at her face. The others fade away. She wills herself into a time-trance and travels to ancient Babylon. She enters the life of one of the original tower builders and addresses a powerful judge, hoping to find forgiveness.*

RUTH: I hear the siren voices of the Tower. The wild beauty of millions of voices drawing me into their labors. And in labor I labor, no time for childbirth, just drop the infant into the apron and back, climbing back, to the beacon. The ascending steps are on the East. The descending steps on the West. One year to the top. If a man falls, if a woman falls, if a child falls, we grieve, quietly, but we do not stop. But if a brick falls we weep, for a brick takes a year to replace. There are whole seasons when the clouds turn an ominous blood red. Perhaps a warning to those among us whose ambition is as dark. It is my fervent wish to ascend to heaven simply to dwell there. But there are those who labor by my side whose intention it is to ascend and serve idols and there are even those who are climbing to wage war with God. Perhaps their cause is just. I know I feel a knot in my throat when they cry the Ancient One slaughtered the entire earth with His flood and we must revolt or we will be His victims again and again. They constantly shoot arrows toward heaven, which, when returning, are seen to be covered with blood. They cry, "We have slain all who are in heaven," but I know they are deluded. I believe that the crafty warrior we are approaching is fortifying their delusions so that He will have the advantage of surprise. Already I have seen evidence of His strategy. My work prospers. I go to lay a brick and two are laid. I go to mortar a row and two are mortared. But those around me falter. The men and women who would worship idols are subject to strange maladies. Some turn into apes and run scrambling and screeching up and down the scaffolding overturning

vats of mortar and hods of brick. Others suffer a horrible plague. Puffing and bloating into strange shapes
like inflated goat bladders they lift off the tower and
are blown away by the wind. Still I climb. Brick after
brick. Climbing, climbing. My hands are a permanent
red from the beautiful bricks burned to a burning. And
still I climb. A woman that I worked alongside happily
for years is gone now. I had said to her, I need more
mortar, and she, like a beast, bellowed these sounds—
Please believe me, I know you must think I am mad to
suggest something without meaning, but these were
the sounds I heard—rafel mahee amek zabi almit. Since
it was impossible that she did not understand me, I re-
peated my words, and she lunged at me with a brick. I
snapped her neck. Nothing will prevent me from reach-
ing heaven.

¶ THE PRISON

The New York Times. Dateline Johannesburg. Three men have
been arrested in connection with the massacre of twenty-six
Black passengers on a commuter train, South Africa's Law and
Order Ministry said today. The Ministry stated that the massacre stems from the battle for supremacy between the African
National Congress and the Zulu organization, Inkatha, during
which nearly eight hundred people have been killed.

> *In the background is heard the Babel text chanted in
> Bantu. The prisoners do a morbid dance with their bars, and
> sing.*

The Song of Walls

They're building more walls
In our invisible prison halls
Than the naked eye can see.
Spinning outside spinning inside
Spinning inside spinning outside
Money's the great divide.

SCENE 5

VICTORY CLIMBING INTO THE JAWS OF DEFEAT

¶ THE HOUSE

JACOB: So here I am itchin to do some of my own climbing. Yes, I'm a climber, climbing, climbing too. And I got my snout sewn into the clouds sniffing for a clue that'll launch me. And I come across this one Yahoo who says that to get really high you first have to get down, so I found myself in the Inferno. We're goin lower and lo and behold we came upon a giant bellowing a chant, RAFEL MAHEE AMEK ZABI ALMIT, and Virgil told Dante this was Nimrod, the king who built the Tower of Babel. Nimrod, oh yes, Nimrod. And so he's condemned to forever babble nonsense, babble babble babble nonsense. It was then I realized the danger that Ruth is in.

RUTH: Jacob! It's happening! Oh Lord, Oh Hashem, Oh Yahweh, don't do... it...
Rafel mahee amek zabi almit
Rafel mahee amek zabi almit
Rafel mahee amek zabi almit

JACOB *scrambles for* The Inferno *and intones Virgil's taunt of Nimrod to exorcise* RUTH. *She chants continuously until he breaks the curse.*

JACOB: "Began a bellowed chant from her brute mouth!"

RUTH: Jacob, rafel how maheee can you amek be so zabi almit!?

JACOB: "Babbling fool, stick to your horn and vent yourself with it when rage or passion stir your stupid soul."

RUTH: You amek, you lousy almit mahee, how dare rafel amek!

JACOB: "Feel there around your neck, you muddle-head, and find the horn there on your overgrown chest!"

RUTH: Keep your smutty mouth off my chest! Oh Lord! Jacob! It stopped.

JACOB: Please forgive me, darling, but if I don't make you angry you don't snap out of it.

RUTH: How dare you call me stupid! I have a condition.

JACOB: That's an understatement. You're a goddamn walking Tower of Babel.

RUTH *and* JACOB *miss like ships in the night.*

JACOB: Pass the milk please.

RUTH: Do you want bitumen for your toast?

> *Long pause*

JACOB: Bitumen?

> *Long pause*

RUTH: What?

> *Long pause*

JACOB: Bitumen. You said bitumen.

RUTH: What's a bitumen?

JACOB: I don't know, you said it.

> *She storms out and he yells to her departing back.*

JACOB: Why won't you trust me? You're not the only one with a secret life!

> *But RUTH has already gone. An impossibly high ladder appears in the center of the living room. Around it the clouds are swirling in all the hues of the sunset. Silent Bedouins gliding out of the wings mysteriously guide JACOB to the base of the ladder.*

JACOB: I want to climb my ladder. I am afraid of falling. But I love to climb. When I climb I enter God's country.

When I climb the air shimmers. When I climb I fuse with the horizon, flatten right out and wrap around three sixty. When I climb my neck prickles and my hackles tickle. When I climb I get that creepy crawly formicative pruriginously itchy sense sensation. When I climb I dream of cornucopic compendiums of corpulent Coptic concubines. Jack in motherfuckers and let's go!

To climb one must know the rungs. Some portion of the brain sends a thought impulse to the nerves which goose the muscles and the leg rises. How high it rises depends on your nerves. If you've got a lot of nerve it goes real high. One, and I mean one, never knows how high is high enough, but that is never the issue when one, and I mean one, is climbing. To climb one must know the terrain and the terrain is voices—once above the clouds you gotta keep your ears peeled for voices, there's millions of them, but whether you can grab one and sing it clean is not a cut and dry question.

First of all, you hafta watch out for God cause the son ofa bitch'll swoop right outa the azure and blindside ya—ram ya just like some battle-barge in Nero's floatin circus. Sometimes he rides a great bird like an Albatross, yellin like Goddamn Idi Amin. And sometimes he strafes you from an ancient test aircraft in his Chuck Yeager outfit screamin profanities like "git outa my envelope you withered tuber." And sometimes he drifts in on these weird figures that look like bloated goat's bladders with gleaming golden eyes. If you get clipped by one of those babies you drop like a rock.

So as I said, it's a matter of getting to know the rungs.

You gotta get real close to them. Maybe set up a work-shop in your dwelling, your shelter, whatever the hell you call it, I don't give a monkey's dick, words are nothin to me, wherever it is you live, and you might not live in your house, I'm trying to say something here about where it is you really live, and I can't come right out and say it because HE: Idi Chuck Yaweh, might be up there listening and he doesn't always stay up there in his lurid little costume dramas. Sometimes he comes down here and mucks about where the people live, so where you live is something you need to play pretty close to the chest.

Now in your workshop you get tight to these rungs. So when you're climbing so high and you caught a voice and you're soaring and those harmonic dissonances are swirling round and the angels are all casting lots to see who's gonna get the first shot at ya, then you're locked in solid to your rungs. You know where you are. Your feet and this object have a magnetic attraction like the two halves of the horizon. You got that groove and you and your ladder are smokin. Rungs are flying by so fast that even the angels trying to grab on are bein thrown off like hobos missin stride on a fast freight. The angels recover instantly and the next thing they'll do is flood the airwaves with mirages.

Their favorite is the Tower of Babel. Beautiful thing. Sight set me reeling first time they sprung it on me. And the sound of those millions of human voices all singin in unison, an ode to joy that made all my nerves flow like the muddy Missisip, just flat out wet myself right there, ejaculated, bled from my ears, the ninety percent of my body that is water reclaimed itself right there, the amphibians crawled back into the sea and the sea rewrote the history right there. But that's just to set you up, because when you're staring at the pinnacle of this tower—your eyeballs a liquid mass—the lightning bolt comes out of some theatrical cloud and shatters every voice in a hundred shards. And all of a sudden it's Swahili and Chinese and Croatian and Balinese and Babylonian and Yoruba and Lithuanian and Portuguese and Sicilian and Mongolian and Finnish and Danish and Zulu and Estonian and Gaelic and your throat seizes up and you blow out like shrapnel tracing cartwheels in seventeen directions like those deadly five pointed throwing disks you see in Bruce Lee movies. They confiscate your ladder. Piles of them in heaven's pound. The memory of your ladder song is something you can't find even if you sift through every Korean deli in Harlem, every pizza joint in Little Italy, every bodega in Hell's Kitchen.

Tap in tight again here because I'm between the lines again: advice on where to pick up memory's shards is harder to come by than God's grace. You see, scuttlebutt scutts it, hearsay hints it, rumor rags it that when one looks on the ruins of this tower one forgets everything one knows. My wife Ruth has resolved that the only way to overcome this horrible confusion of tongues is to secretly rebuild the tower. She thinks that I don't know of her plan. She's even more secretive than I am, but I discovered her dream because of the very porous state of mind that floats over our heads as we sleep. And secretly, I wish her Godspeed. Because when she succeeds in constructing her new Tower brick by brick within her mind and then springs it full blown, full built, then the Lord, the goddamn landlord of the envelope, will be forced to come to the table. Forced to negotiate. We want to be in Paradise. We want it. We deserve it. You bet your ass, it's Hubris. And about time. How many millennium we gonna scrape around the humble pen? You heard the story? Said it himself, "Behold, they are one people, and they all have one language; and nothing they propose to do will now be impossible for them." Hear that?!!!!! Do you hear that? Anything we can imagine, we can do. Well, I say, tap in, jack in, and get tight with those rungs, because I'm ready to climb.

A squadron of angels dive bombs JACOB, *and, like a flying Wallenda, he evades each wave.* RUTH *returns, dictionary in hand, unaware of the angels, and is alarmed by* JACOB's *behavior.*

RUTH: Jacob! What are you doing!

The angels exit, wings twitching with annoyance.

JACOB: Nothing dear, just chatting with my guardian angels.

RUTH: I found it. "Bitumen"—it's tar or asphalt, earthy pitchy stuff, mortar.

JACOB: Didn't you tell me this once before?

RUTH: When? [*now alarmed*] When?

¶ THE OPERATING THEATRE

RAFEL: Check the respirator.

ZABI: She's starting to come to. Increase anesthetic.

AMEK: Increased.

JACOB: Breathe deep, breathe deep, that's it.

ZABI: Taking it in.

RAFEL: Eyes glazed.

ZABI: She's under again.

> *She's losing consciousness, lightly, softly.*

RUTH: Falling.

RUTH, JACOB, RAFEL, AMEK, ZABI: The tower rises.

RUTH: Falling.

AMEK: Neck bristles.

RUTH: Falling.

RAFEL: Sweet sweat.

ZABI: Wet sweet wet.

RUTH, JACOB, RAFEL, AMEK, ZABI: The tower rises.

RUTH: Where's my body?

AMEK: Sweet body.

RAFEL: Sweat body.

ZABI: Falling bodies.

RUTH, JACOB, RAFEL, AMEK, ZABI: The tower rises.

RUTH: Rising.

RUTH, JACOB, RAFEL, AMEK, ZABI: Rising.

RUTH: Rising.

> *Now that she's completely under, a violent argument begins.*

ZABI: An operating theatre. I am on the table.

RUTH: *I* am on the table!

ZABI: Yes, on the table.

RUTH: Stop taking my voice!

ZABI: We're all the same voice.

RUTH: No! It's a trap!

RAFEL: Where am I?

RUTH: Is this a prison?

ZABI: There's no way out!

RAFEL: Kabul? Sarajevo?

RUTH: How do I do that How do they do that
　　　How do I do that How do they…

AMEK: [*as* RUTH *repeats*] How do I do that How do they do
　　　that.

RUTH: As fast as thought.

RAFEL: I hear my thoughts in other mouths.

AMEK: My mouth is disappearing.

RAFEL: We lose the West Bank we'll be destroyed.

JACOB: No. Leveraged buyouts are good for the economy.

RUTH: Then who put me in this cell?

JACOB: False prophets.

RAFEL: False profits.

RUTH: I remember that.

RAFEL: How do I remember that?

JACOB: It's a convulsion.

AMEK: A takeover boom.

RUTH: I want out I want out I want out I want out I want out.

ZABI: She's not going to make it.

RAFEL: Transfer the unit, goddamnit!

RUTH: I need more mortar.

JACOB: Slam the cell, it's the SEC.

JACOB, ZABI: Rafel mahee amek zabi almit.

RUTH: I'm gonna break out I'm gonna break out!

ZABI: There's no way out that way!

RUTH: You're wrong!

RUTH, JACOB, AMEK, RAFEL: WE BREAK NOW!

> *Suddenly,* RUTH *is isolated in the light. Everyone else*

fades away.

RUTH: How I was born to this cell I'll never know, but all of a
sudden there I was, the striped suit, the blaring
klaxons—Arrooogah, Arroogah, and those leering
German Shepherds. It coulda been anywhere, I didn't
know, so I started watching the way the water went
down the drain. That would at least give me the right
hemisphere, but I realized I was already entirely in the
right hemisphere and the water rushing down always
made me think of God. And it very well coulda been
God who kept changing the sound outside the walls.
Sometimes it sounded tropical like it coulda been San
Salvador. And sometimes I heard this hot desert wind
and it coulda been Baghdad. When I was nightshipped
in I was unconscious so I figure my disorientation is
Someone's idea of strategic. I see no one. Occasionally
I hear shrieks from what must be other prisoners, but I
never decipher their languages. Words drift in through
the food slot on all kinds of voices. Barrel chested meat
butchers, the divas cackling in Mozart's Prague, the
eunuchs in the seraglio—greed oozing from every one
of their vowels, even an odd angel or two snagged in
the wax (they whisper that in the beginning there were
only consonants—and God's gift to Man in the garden
was vowels—The Lord giveth and the Lord laugheth
all the way to the bank—try laughing without vowels). What are the stories they're trying to tell? There's
the one with the file in the cake, there's the one about
the gun out of soap, there's the one about hiding inside the corpse. Every story they sing ends in death so

every night in my cell, not that I know when night folds me in its iron maiden's bosom—lights always flashing in here like a pinball morgue—I plan my escape. I'm building a tower and climbing out. Every night, all night, I scratch the bricks of the cell. Hardening my nails for the climbing.

¶ THE PRISON

The Wall Street Journal. Dateline the Gaza Strip. A Palestinian youth was killed and thirty-eight others were wounded as Arab residents of the West Bank and Gaza Strip struck to protest a surge of killings by Israeli troops acting under tough measures to quell the uprising called the Intifadah.

> *In the background is heard the Babel text in Arabic. The prisoners attempt to break out. Standing on top of each other's shoulders they try to scale the bars. They sing.*

The Break Out Song

All we want is to break out
of the bondage of money and doubt!

SCENE 6

THE BOOK OF SLIPPAGE

¶ THE HOUSE

RUTH: Jacob, I want you to play Nimrod.

JACOB: What is this, some new sex fantasy?

RUTH: No, I need help on my project, but I can't explain. Not yet.

JACOB: Just what is this project, Ruth? Is it connected to the government?

RUTH: If I let the idea out of my own mind there'll be leaks.

JACOB: I can keep a secret.

RUTH: I know you can. It's not that you would say anything… it's… slippage.

JACOB: Slippage?

RUTH: Yes, you remember my last project, *The Book of Slippage*? Things get in the air, then like in aerodynamics they develop resistance and accidents happen, a constant slipstream of accidents. So forgive me, but I'm not letting anything into the air. I'm going to be my own wind tunnel.

JACOB: All right, what's my costume? Georgio Armani three piece? Sharkskin zoot suit? Golden caftan?

RUTH: Ya nailed it on the last one. Nimrod was the King who built the Tower of Babel, the tower of... yes... the Tower of... Babel... of...
[*stammering*]
Ba... bel
Ba bel
Ba bel
Ba bel

JACOB: Ruth!

¶ THE OPERATING THEATRE

AMEK: The heart rate just went sky high.

RAFEL: I don't know what we're looking at here.

ZABI: Her tongue's convulsing!

JACOB: Doctor, I'm shaking all over. What's happening!?

The operating room explodes like a revivalist meeting.

RUTH: Nimrod, Nimrod, Nimrod, was also the great grandson of Noah.

AMEK: Noah, Noah.

ZABI: And talk about sins of the fathers. The sins of the fathers.

RAFEL: Nimrod's granddaddy Ham came upon his father, Noah.

ZABI: Granddaddy Ham, Granddaddy Ham, Nimrod's Granddaddy Ham.

JACOB: Came upon his father, Noah,

AMEK: Noah, Noah.

JACOB: In the tent, passed out naked in a drunken stupor.

RUTH: Ham went and told his brothers that Dad was hanging out in the tent.

RUTH, JACOB, RAFEL, AMEK, ZABI: Oh Dad, Ohhh Dad was a hanging out.

RUTH: So the two bro took a sheepskin, and laid it upon both their shoulders, and went backwards and covered the nakedness of their father.

JACOB, RAFEL, ZABI: And covered the nakedness, the nakedness, of their father.

RUTH: Now

JACOB: Now

RAFEL: Now

AMEK: Now

ZABI: [*screaming*] Now!

RUTH: Now the story gets a little murky. It seems that Noah wakes up and realizes that Ham has done something to him, and so he curses Ham's son Canaan to be a slave.

JACOB: A slave

RAFEL: Curses, he curses

AMEK: Ham's son Canaan

ZABI: To be. A slave.

RUTH: But what the hell did Ham do wrong?

JACOB: All he did was see his dad naked.

RAFEL: How does Noah know that anything's happened?

AMEK: He got a sore asshole when he was nappin?

ZABI: This some accusation of incest?

RUTH: Why mince words? Call it like it is.

RUTH: Right here in the bible is a justification of slavery!

JACOB: Slavery   RAFEL: Slavery

AMEK: Slavery   ZABI: Justification

AMEK: And why?

ZABI: Why?

RAFEL: A punishment for a son seeing his father naked?

ZABI: What!! How can that be?!

AMEK: Oh it don't really mean *that*.
       The Good Book's talkin 'bout incest.

RUTH, JACOB, RAFEL, AMEK: It means incest, incest, incest.

ZABI: But if we sing it as a tale of incest, then it's really a mangle
       because how are we supposed to untangle the truth
       when it's veiled, veiled,
       veiled in double speak?
       O double double speak.

RUTH: So now you know what's brewing in Nimrod's mind.

RAFEL: The son of a slave.

AMEK: Maybe he wanted revenge.

ZABI: But maybe he was pure of heart
      and wanted to wipe all that away
      and walk with God again.

RUTH: He began to be a mighty one on the earth.

RAFEL: A mighty one.

RUTH, AMEK: He was a mighty hunter before the Lord.

RAFEL: Before the Lord.

RUTH, AMEK, ZABI: And the beginning of his kingdom was,

RAFEL: The beginning was,

RUTH, JACOB, RAFEL, AMEK, ZABI: [*crescendo*] Babel Babel
      Babel!

JACOB: Ruth!

RUTH: Yes?

JACOB: Nothing is gonna be impossible for us now!

RUTH: But beware of slippage and do not speak.

RAFEL: Absolute silence and there'll be no leak.

AMEK, ZABI: A song of silence to the Tower's peak.

¶ THE PRISON

New York Times. Dateline Srinagar, Kashmir. Indian troops burned down four hundred houses and killed at least twenty people in the town of Handwara, said Indian reporters at the scene. The troops from the paramilitary Border Security Force were said to have been retaliating after a grenade was thrown by a Kashmiri guerrilla.

> *In the background is heard the Babel text in Hindi.*
> RUTH'*s head is bound by a black hood. The prisoners sing.*

The Song of Censorship

We must not speak. We must not see,
Jailer says
There's only one reality,
Jailer says.
If I want your opinion
I will give it to you.
So we must not speak. We must not see
There's more than one reality.

SCENE 7

Sɪᴍᴏᴏɴ

¶ THE HOUSE

Rᴜᴛʜ: Do you feel anything?

Jᴀᴄᴏʙ: What is that, an invitation to fight?

Rᴜᴛʜ: No, no, do you feel a presence, like this strange presence, in the house?

Jᴀᴄᴏʙ: No.

Rᴜᴛʜ: Don't just dismiss it like that. Give it a chance.

Jᴀᴄᴏʙ: I'm sorry. Why don't I see if I can hunt down this…
[*suddenly confounded*]
…TOOOOOWWWEERRRR…OF…MORTAL
COILS…
No! I'm in BIG trouble making my words COME.
[who is moving my lips?]
EXCEPT IN SIMOONS OF MORTAL COILS.
… DID YOU DO THIS?!!

69

RUTH: What did you say—you said—
    HERE...COMES...THE BIG ONE!

> *Twisters are coming from three directions, lightning flashes, and a large white fist fills the air. Three small cones of sand form across the stage as if hourglasses were draining slowly from above.*

¶ THE OPERATING THEATRE

RUTH: I am on the table. Of destruction.

ZABI: Three hundred and forty years of simoons, sand whipping storms.

JACOB, RAFEL, AMEK, ZABI: What is this wind?

RUTH: Is it the presence of the Lord?

JACOB, RAFEL, AMEK, ZABI: What is this wind?

JACOB: Is it the sound of our language blowing away?

RUTH: How long must we walk through this wind
    before we reach the Doctor's mind?

JACOB: Who is speaking?

RUTH: How can I have lost my way?
    How can I have lost my way?

When all I must remember
is to lift my head.
[*pause*]
Yes, now I can feel my blood memory rushing back to
    me.

    At the surface the surgeons warn of heart attack.

ZABI: Looks like cardiac arrest.

AMEK: Heart rate blue line.

RAFEL: CPR fast. Conductors. Current. Hurry. Vital signs.

AMEK: None.

RAFEL: Again. Conductors. Current. Vital signs.

AMEK: No movement.

JACOB: KEEP TRYING.

RAFEL: Again. Try it here.

JACOB: Ruth, please, don't die.

RAFEL: Conductors. Up voltage. Current. Vital signs. Vital
    signs. Give me vital signs. Damn it!

AMEK: [*long pause*] None.

pause

RAFEL: She's gone. We're sorry. We did everything we could. We're sorry.

JACOB: Noooooooooooooo...> [*He collapses*]

pause

Back inside RUTH'S *mind*

RAFEL, AMEK, ZABI: [*a clear, meditative tone, sustaining*] Ooooooooooo ...

RUTH: I am levitating on the table.

RUTH, JACOB: I've been silent for so long I've focused enormous energy.

RUTH, JACOB, RAFEL, AMEK, ZABI: I can feel the thrill coursing through my body,
the shivers and tremors.

RUTH: And I start to rise.

RUTH, AMEK: I am above it.

RUTH: Floating above it.

RUTH, ZABI: I can see my body below on the table.

RUTH, RAFEL: I can see a tunnel with a bright white light at
the end.

RUTH, JACOB: Or is it a tower?

RUTH, AMEK: I don't know if I am moving up or across. There
are no dimensions here.

RUTH: A prayer, my motion is a prayer.

RUTH, ZABI: Drifting in prayer, I catapult and somersault
through the air.

RUTH: Almighty God, I love thee.

> RUTH *leaves the operating table and stands alone.*

RUTH: After years of building, brick by brick, I broke through
the skin of heaven with my tower. And there, hovering
above the pinnacle—about six inches—floating on what
looked like the shimmers above asphalt roads in heat
waves, was a temple with a hot pink marble gate. I
lunged at the gate and there He was—The Lord. A long
white man with a long white beard rising from a long
white chaise lounge. His eyes were ghosting like black
pearls and his teeth… he broke into a broad grin at the
sight of me… The Teeth… The Teeth… were not white
but brass. I was dazzled by their razor sharp points and
I think He knew they were one of His best features.
"Good Evening," He said, "would you care for a cock-
tail?" "No thank you," I shot back, "I'd rather wrestle."

Like an ancient Fred Astaire, He glided across the threshold and clapped me in a full-nelson. I felt his hot breath scorch the back of my neck and I knew every gazelle on the Serengetti ever fallen upon by excellent hyenas. "My angel," He crooned, and I could feel this powerful wraith getting the horn. I slammed my heel down on his foot and he let out a howl like a demon in the Chinese Opera. "Nice move, you flatulent funambulist," I spit, as I snaked out of his grip, "but not yet." I gave him a ramming head butt to the solar plexus but even as I heard the breath fly out of him he dissolved in a fog and I felt this burning sensation in my ass. Yahweh, the Angry Avenging God, was trying to bugger me in His spirit form. I was thrashing around on twenty-five hot feet desperately trying to clamp down this mist tunneling up my ass. There was only one thing I knew He'd fall for—I'd have to pretend to submit. "Forgive me Lord, I don't know what got into me, Oh Hashem, please set me free and I will worship you." That gets em every time. Pfffffftt—there He was, rubbing His hands like a fly. *Long* fingers. "Now my child," He commanded, "assume the position." I got down on all fours and looking back between my legs I watched Him approach. Longest shlong I ever saw, the prime patriarchal part, a real biblical number. In a flash, I whirled, and one hand grabbed the frightful head and one hand that awful wrinkled sack. He exploded with a deadly babel of curses in Swahili and Chinese and Croatian, and Balinese and Babylonian and Yoruba, and Lithuanian and Portuguese and Sicilian, and Mongolian and Finnish and Danish, and Zulu and Estonian and Gaelic and it must have been my fist clenched around His nuts that blocked Him from dematerializing because we started whirling around and around like those hot desert whirlwinds the Bedouins call simoons. We got huge, swelling up so big we bloated all five kingdoms of heaven. Then we'd tornado the other way, shrinking like water down a drain until the tear drop of a locust loomed as large as the Dead Sea. All this time, I don't know if I'm awake or asleep, I just keep mouthing, "I want to be in Paradise. I want to be in Paradise. I want to be… " I lost track of time. Many times I think I fainted. I saw visions of nomads moving through the desert with long camel trains. My mind kept wandering to the Hanging Gardens and then I'd suffer the hammering of hundreds of fists, like nomadic drummers, on my mouth and ears, bruising them to pulp. Then I heard the sound of a distant train, mournful, haunting, beautiful—was it the far voice of God?— and I found myself on the operating table—Jacob saying, "Breathe deep, breathe deep, that's it… breathe deep, that's it… "

THE PRISON

Wall Street Journal. Dateline Kabul. Afghan guerrillas fired a rocket into Kabul killing six people and wounding nineteen.

> *In the background is heard the Babel text in Russian. The operating table has elevated to a height of seven feet. The prisoners wrap it with prison bars.* RUTH *clambers up into the structural supports beneath the table.* JACOB *follows.*

SCENE 8

DISPERSION

¶ THE HOUSE

> RUTH *and* JACOB *are swinging upside down by their knees from the underside of the towering operating table. They're attempting to laugh so as not to scream.* RAFEL, AMEK *and* ZABI *stand in the living room like a Greek chorus.*

RUTH: Jacob! The house is on fire!

RAFEL, AMEK, ZABI: What is this wind?

JACOB: The garden's a bonfire!

RAFEL, AMEK, ZABI: Rafel mahee amek zabi almit.

RUTH: The television's exploding!

RAFEL, AMEK, ZABI: What is this wind?

JACOB: The toilet's an inferno!

RAFEL, AMEK, ZABI: Rafel mahee amek zabi almit.

RUTH: Look at the pink flamingos! Blazing!

RAFEL, AMEK, ZABI: What is this wind?

RUTH: Jacob, I can't see! The wind's seared my eyes!

RAFEL, AMEK, ZABI: Rafel mahee amek zabi almit. [*repeating sotto voce*]

JACOB: You hear that riveting sound?!!

RUTH: Oh no, I'm falling…

JACOB: Every word is shattering into its alphabet.

RUTH: I'm falling…

JACOB: The air is swirling with jagged D's and razor sharp L's, and boomeranging V's combining with each other more rapidly than words froth in the idiot savant's mouth. An orgy of alphabets cross pollinating, the Hebrew mating with the Greek, the Egyptian hieroglyphic with the Cirillian.

RUTH: Falling…

JACOB: When we're hit by this bolt of sound our hearts are going to burst with the sound of a thousand choirs.

RUTH: The sky blackened with falling bodies.

JACOB: This is the end of the Tower. The end!

RUTH: No! Walk three days in the shadow of the ruins. Meet me at the sound of a distant train.

JACOB: I can't! RUTH! You have to stop!

RUTH: I'm going to build!

¶ THE OPERATING THEATRE

AMEK: Doctor, look at this! The heart rate's coming back!

RAFEL: Oh my God, I don't believe it!

JACOB: Yes, yes, please!

ZABI: She's been gone three minutes. It's impossible!

RAFEL: Oxygen fast. We're going in.

Running from the Apocalypse

ZABI: I can't hold a thought.

AMEK: As it forms it fades.

RAFEL: The thought breaks.

ZABI: Cracking.

JACOB, AMEK: Running.

JACOB, AMEK, ZABI: They are running.

RUTH, JACOB, RAFEL, AMEK, ZABI: Huge masses running.

RAFEL: Pulsing with voices,
  a choir of seventy angels,
  all singing as they cast lots
  to destroy our tongues.

AMEK: What a divine cacophony.

RUTH: As I wander over the dunes
  I see the seventy.
  Wandering, wandering,
  I see the seventy.

AMEK: An angel to destroy the tongue of Japheth.

ZABI: An angel to destroy the tongue of Ham.

JACOB: An angel to destroy the tongue of Shem.

RUTH, JACOB, RAFEL, AMEK, ZABI: Seventy angels for seventy tongues.

RUTH: I see the seventy
  as I wander the ruins

of this scarred and babbling tower.

Avenging angels stride in a continuous file past the operating table, some of them battle weary, some with swords raised.

¶ THE PRISON

The Chicago Tribune. Dateline Miami. Violence in Miami ebbed after two nights of rioting in the mostly Black Overtown and Liberty City areas. The riots touched off by the fatal shooting of a Black motorcyclist by a Hispanic policeman, highlighted increasing tensions between the Black and Hispanic…

The other prisoners attack RUTH *and she fends them off with a trowel. Alone and in disgust, she hurls the trowel to the ground.*

SCENE 9

BABEL

¶ THE HOUSE

> RUTH *pulls* JACOB *into the ruins of their burnt home. The chairs are still smoldering.*

JACOB: Ruth, a third of the house is burnt to the ground, the back third was swallowed in the earth, and so what if the living room's still standing—what the hell are we doing here?!

RUTH: In this room will rise the new Tower of Babel. Please, come with me.

JACOB: That tower is in ruins and its builder is buried to the waist in the eighth circle. For god's sake, break off this insane plan.

RUTH: I have rebuilt it.

JACOB: Whoever looks upon those ruins forgets everything they know.

RUTH: What?

JACOB: Ruth?

RUTH: What?

JACOB: Ruth! Speak to me!

> *She starts a droning mesmerizing chant.*

RUTH: Walk for three days in the shadow of the tower,
  three days without ever leaving it,
  three of falling,
  falling in the shadow of the three days,
  three days of shadow,
  days and days of shadows falling,
  the falling days,
  the shadow days…
  CALL THE HOSPITAL, JACOB!
  … three shadows…

JACOB: Oh lord, Ruth, just sit there. Don't fall! I'm calling an
  ambulance.

RUTH: … falling in threes, shadows of three, ever three,
  ever shadows, shadows, shadows…

¶ The Operating Theatre

RUTH, JACOB, RAFEL, AMEK, ZABI: The scene is an operating theatre.

I am on the table.

RUTH: I am waking…

JACOB: … waking…

AMEK: … waking…

RUTH: I hear my heart beating, booming in my ears.

ZABI: The operation complete.

AMEK: Anesthetic lapping thin.

JACOB: The room is wearing quiet.

AMEK: I can hear the sound of ruins of bricks crumbling to dust.

RAFEL: No, it is not that.

ZABI: I can hear the solid sounds of shoes on the floor.

RUTH, JACOB, RAFEL, AMEK, ZABI: And the breath of those
hovering around me.

RUTH: No, it is my breath.

AMEK: No, it is the breath of the respirator.

RUTH: I thought I heard the sound of a choir of seventy angels
but it must have been my imagination wandering, wan-

dering, wandering…

RAFEL: That's it. Finish up. Gauze wrap double weight. Take over, Doctor.

> *As* RUTH *regains consciousness she touches the heavy bandages on her mouth.*

JACOB: It's all right. It's over now. Don't try to talk.

RAFEL: She's going to be fine. She's strong.
You can go with her to recovery, but make sure she sleeps.

> RUTH *tries to say "a choir…"*

JACOB: Shhh… Doctor says you're gonna be fine, just fine.

> RUTH *tries to say "the Tower…"*

JACOB: Shhh… Doctor says I can take you to recovery. You're gonna be all right. You're gonna live till you're a hundred and eight. But you're gonna need a lot of rest. Go to sleep…

> RUTH *drops off to sleep for an instant as if moving through a passage. The others fade away and she rises from the table removing the bandages from her mouth. This speech starts as a lament for all those lost and ends as a revery of personal victory.*

RUTH: Like refugees we lined up outside what had been our tower, now transformed into chambers of forgetting. A third of it had been sunken into the ground, a third had been burnt, and a third was left standing. Everyone who looked upon the ruins began to forget. There was a chamber for each person and after sleeping forty days and forty nights the slate was blank. There was no choice. To drive from our minds the sound of that onslaught we had to forget everything we knew. Most of us did forget and live in relative peace. Haunted by a feeling of dull remorse, but out of the path of that howling chaos.

But there are a few,
and I am one,
who never forgot.
I contained the memory,
wrapping the pain in layers, over and over,
so that it became
like a pearl.

RUTH *places a pearl on her tongue. Beside her,* JACOB *wrestles with an angel. Lights fade.*

The End

AMERICAN THEATER IN LITERATURE (ATL)

Established by The Contemporary Arts Educational Project, Inc., a nonprofit corporation, and published through its Sun & Moon Press, the American Theater in Literature program was established to promote American theater as a literary form and to educate readers about contemporary and modern theater. The program publishes work of major American playwrights as well as younger, developing dramatists in various publishing programs of the Press, including Mark Taper Forum Plays (plays selected and produced by the Mark Taper Forum in Los Angeles), the Sun & Moon Classics (collections of plays of international significance) and as a regular imprint of Sun & Moon Press.

Books in this Program

Len Jenkin *Dark Ride and Other Plays*
(Sun & Moon Classics: 22)
Robert Auletta *The Persians*
(A Mark Taper Forum Play)
Matthew Maguire *The Tower*
Kier Peters *The Confirmation*

Other Books of Theater from Sun & Moon Press

Mac Wellman, ed. *Theatre of Wonders:*
Six Contemporary American Plays
(Plays by Len Jenkin, Jeffrey Jones
Des McAnuff, Elizabeth Wray and Mac Wellman)
Mac Wellman *The Professional Frenchman*
(A Blue Corner Book)
Mac Wellman *Bad Penny*
(A Blue Corner Book)

Douglas Messerli *Silence All Round Marked:*
An Historical Play in Hysteria Writ
(A Blue Corner Book)
Jerome Lawrence *A Golden Circle*